Sta[illegible]

Paper 9

Financial Reporting

British Library Cataloguing-in-Publication Data

A catalogue record for this book is available from the British Library.

Published by AT Foulks Lynch Ltd
Number 4
The Griffin Centre
Staines Road
Feltham
Middlesex
TW14 0HS

ISBN 0 7483 3240 5

PREFACE

ynchpins are the most exciting product in recent years for CIMA students. ased on our highly successful Examination Notes, Lynchpins are the onvenient way to revise - anytime - anywhere.

ynchpins cover the syllabus thoroughly. They are not just a checklist of topics learn but rather cover the key points with succinct detail which will bring the opics back to the front of your mind.

iagrams and worked examples all help the revision process.

he books are pocket sized - but they pack a big punch.

CONTENTS

apter 1 ***Published accounts disclosure requirements***

THE PROFIT AND LOSS ACCOUNT

Introduction

e prescribed form of accounts is laid down by *Sch 4 CA 1985*, and enacts the uirements of the EC fourth directive. A choice of format is given: four for profit and loss account and two for the balance sheet. Once a company has de its choice of formats it should normally continue with these from one year the next year.

e different profit and loss account formats give different information. Format analyses on an operational basis; format 2 analyses costs by type of penditure. Formats 3 and 4 disclose the same information as formats 1 and 2 t allow the presentation of profit and loss accounts in horizontal form. They uld not normally be used by UK companies. Balance sheet format 1 is a ntinuous vertical format; while format 2 sets out firstly all assets, followed by liabilities, which would allow for a horizontal format. The formats used in up accounts will be considered later.

Format 1, the 'operational' format

Turnover
Cost of sales
Gross profit or loss
Distribution costs
Administrative expenses
Other operating income
Income from shares in group undertakings
Income from participating interests
Income from other fixed asset investments
Other interest receivable and similar income
Amounts written off investments

---

tes

12. Interest payable and similar charges
13. Tax on profit or loss on ordinary activities
14. Profit or loss on ordinary activities after taxation
15. Extraordinary income
16. Extraordinary charges
17. Extraordinary profit or loss
18. Tax on extraordinary profit or loss
19. Other taxes not shown under the above items
20. Profit or loss for the financial year

1.3 Format 2, the 'type of expenditure' format

1. Turnover
2. Change in stocks of finished goods and work in progress
3. Own work capitalised
4. Other operating income
5. (a) Raw materials and consumables
   (b) Other external charges
6. Staff costs:
   (a) Wages and salaries
   (b) Social security costs
   (c) Other pension costs
7. (a) Depreciation and other amounts written off tangible a intangible fixed assets
   (b) Exceptional amounts written off current assets
8. Other operating charges
9. Income from shares in group undertakings
10. Income from participating interests
11. Income from other fixed asset investments
12. Other interest receivable and similar income
13. Amounts written off investments
14. Interest payable and similar charges

Notes

Tax on profit or loss on ordinary activities
Profit or loss on ordinary activities after taxation
Extraordinary income
Extraordinary charges
Extraordinary profit or loss
Tax on extraordinary profit or loss
Other taxes not shown under the above items
Profit or loss for the financial year

4 Comments on the profit and loss account

As every item on the formats is prefixed by an arabic number, they can all be combined if either immaterial individually or such combination would help assessment of the profit and loss account.

Where items are combined, the individual amounts must be disclosed in a note to the accounts.

PROFIT AND LOSS ACCOUNT - ACCOUNTING PRINCIPLES AND DISCLOSURE REQUIREMENTS

General principles

Formats 3 and 4

Horizontal versions of formats 1 and 2 respectively. Rarely used

Show cost of sales, distribution and admin expenses after depreciation

Disclose depreciation charges shown in formats 2 and 4 in a note where formats 1 and 3 used

Disclose on face of profit and loss account

Profit or loss on ordinary activities before taxation
Transfers to and from reserves
Dividends paid and proposed

tes

- It has also become common practice to disclose an 'Operating profit' c the face of the profit and loss account, being the gross profit le operating expenses, but before interest payable/receivable.

2.2 Example profit and loss account in format 1

SPECIMEN PLC

Profit and loss account for the year ended 31 March 19X6
(Presented in vertical style)

	£'00
Turnover	11,13
Cost of sales	(8,46
Gross profit	2,67
Distribution costs	(44
Administrative expenses	(1,50
Other operating costs/income	(11
Operating profit	60
Investment income	1
Interest payable and similar charges	(8
Profit on ordinary activities before taxation	53
Tax on profit on ordinary activities	(24
Profit on ordinary activities after taxation	28
Dividends	(16
Retained profit for the financial year	12

Movements on reserves are set out in note X

Notes

THE BALANCE SHEET

Format 1

Called up share capital not paid (1)

Fixed assets

I Intangible assets

1. Development costs
2. Concessions, patents, licences, trade marks and similar rights and assets
3. Goodwill
4. Payments on account

II Tangible assets

1. Land and buildings
2. Plant and machinery
3. Fixtures, fittings, tools and equipment
4. Payments on account and assets in course of construction

III Investments

1. Shares in group undertakings
2. Loans to group undertakings
3. Participating interests
4. Loans to undertakings in which the company has a participating interest
5. Other investments other than loans
6. Other loans
7. Own shares

C. Current assets

I Stocks

1. Raw materials and consumables
2. Work in progress
3. Finished goods and goods for resale
4. Payments on account

II Debtors

1. Trade debtors
2. Amounts owed by group undertakings
3. Amounts owed by undertakings in which t company has a participating interest
4. Other debtors
5. Called up share capital not paid (1)
6. Prepayments and accrued income (2)

III Investments

1. Shares in group undertakings
2. Own shares
3. Other investments

IV Cash at bank and in hand

D. Prepayments and accrued income (2)

E. Creditors: amounts falling due within one year

1. Debenture loans
2. Bank loans and overdrafts
3. Payments received on account
4. Trade creditors
5. Bills of exchange payable

Notes

6. Amounts owed to group undertakings
7. Amounts owed to undertakings in which the company has a participating interest
8. Other creditors including taxation and social security
9. Accruals and deferred income (3)

Net current assets (liabilities)

Total assets less current liabilities

Creditors: amounts falling due after more than one year

1. Debenture loans
2. Bank loans and overdrafts
3. Payments received on account
4. Trade creditors
5. Bills of exchange payable
6. Amounts owed to group undertakings
7. Amounts owed to undertakings in which the company has a participating interest
8. Other creditors including taxation and social security
9. Accruals and deferred income (3)

Provisions for liabilities and charges

1. Pensions and similar obligations
2. Taxation, including deferred taxation
3. Other provisions

Accruals and deferred income (3)

Capital and reserves

I Called up share capital

II Share premium account

---

tes

III Revaluation reserve

IV Other reserves

1. Capital redemption reserve
2. Reserve for own shares
3. Reserves provided for by the articles of association
4. Other reserves

V Profit and loss account

Notes on the balance sheet formats

(1) Called up share capital not paid

(Items A and C.II.5.)
This item may be shown in either of the two positions given.

(2) Prepayments and accrued income

(Items C.II.6 and D.)
This item may be shown in either of the two positions given.

(3) Accruals and deferred income

(Items E.9 and H.9 and J.)
The two positions given for this item at E.9 and H.9 are an alternative to the position at J, but if the item is not shown in a position corresponding to that at J it may be shown in either or both of the other two positions (as the case may require).

Notes

2 **Comments on the balance sheet**

Items on formats prefixed by an arabic number can be combined if either

immaterial individually, or

helps assessment of state of affairs or result for year - disclose detail in note

Items on formats prefixed by capital letter or roman numeral must be shown on the face of the balance sheet unless nil both years

Change in format from prior year only if special reasons (which must be disclosed)

Comparatives to be given. Where not comparative, adjust, and give explanation

CA requirements are minimum disclosures

BALANCE SHEET ITEMS - ACCOUNTING PRINCIPLES AND DISCLOSURE REQUIREMENTS

1 **Accounting principles for the balance sheet**

Accounting policies must be disclosed where relevant

CA85 contains accounting principles to be followed in determining each balance sheet amount. These encapsulate best accounting practice

otes

4.2 Example balance sheet in format 1

SPECIMEN PLC

Balance sheet at 31 March 19X6

	£'000	£'00
Fixed assets		
Intangible assets		28
Tangible assets		1,30
Investments		29
		1,87
Current assets		
Stocks	839	
Debtors		66
Investments	70	
Cash at bank and in hand	109	
	1,687	
Creditors: amounts falling due within one year	(834)	
Net current assets		85
Total assets less current liabilities		2,73
Creditors: amounts falling due after more than one year	(600)	
Provisions for liabilities and charges	(179)	
Accruals and deferred income	(382)	
		(1,16
		1,56

Notes

apital and reserves	£'000
Called up share capital	600
Share premium account	270
Revaluation reserve	280
Profit and loss account	419
	1,569

gned
Giles (Chairman)
July 19X6

THE DIRECTORS' REPORT

1 Required contents of the directors' report

emember the mnemonic

rectors' names and interests in shares and debentures

demnity insurance

eview

nployees

aritable and political donations

ansactions in fixed assets

itlook

esults

ares - own purchase

---

tes

Research and development

Events after the balance sheet date

Principal activity

Open market value of land and buildings

Reappointment of auditors

Transfers to reserves and dividends

Signature

6 OPERATING AND FINANCIAL REVIEW

6.1 Introduction

The ASB recommended in 1993 that the accounts of large companies shou contain an Operating and Financial Review (OFR). This should help no specialist users to understand the message of the accounts, but is non-mandato guidance on recommended best practice.

6.2 Contents of an OFR

- Operating review

  discuss the results for the period

  discuss investments to meet future needs and challenges

- Financial review

  the capital structure of the business
  treasury policies adopted
  cash flow and current liquidity
  other factors relevant to the current and future financing needs

---

Notes

STATUTORY ACCOUNTS: SPECIAL REPORTING SITUATIONS

1 Abbreviated accounts for small and medium-sized companies

Criteria

	Small	*Medium*
Turnover	£2.8m	£11.2m
Gross assets	£1.4m	£5.6m
Average employees	50	250

Qualification

Satisfy two criteria in both current and preceding year

Lose qualification if fail to satisfy the criteria for two consecutive years

Filing exemptions

	Small	*Medium*
Directors' report	Not required	Required in full
Profit and loss account	Not required	Abbreviated - may commence with gross profit
Balance sheets	Abbreviated - main headings only	Required in full
Notes	Abbreviated - limited information required	Abbreviated - analysis of turnover not required

otes

- Annual reports to members

  If small company then can send less detailed report to **members**

  Face of balance sheet and profit and loss account virtually the same

  Less detailed notes and directors' report

- A company is ineligible if it is

  A public limited company

  A banking or insurance company

  An authorised person under the *FSA 1986*

  A member of a group containing an ineligible company

8 THE CADBURY REPORT

8.1 Introduction

- 'Report of the committee on the financial aspects of corpora governance' chaired by Sir Adrian Cadbury was published in Decemb 1992.

- UK listed companies are required to comply with the code in the annual report or else explain their non-compliance.

8.2 The Code of best practice

- **Covers four areas**

  the board of directors (role and content)
  non-executive directors
  executive directors
  reporting and controls (including an audit committee)

Notes

SSAPs AND FRSs. THE DEARING REVIEW

e current system for issuing Financial Reporting Standards (FRSs) was eloped by the Dearing committee after the Dearing Report of September 38. There are four separate bodies:

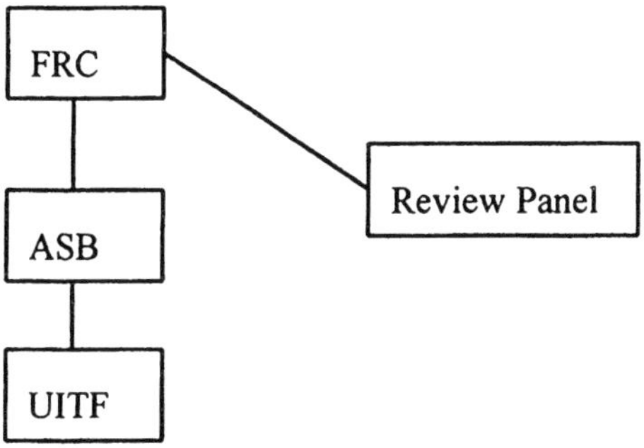

THE WORKINGS OF THE FRC, THE ASB, THE UITF AND THE REVIEW PANEL

Standard setting procedure

Financial Reporting Council (FRC)

approximately 25 members - all sections of industry/profession/public sector

Responsible for

- Broad policy issues
- Direction of work of ASB

- Accounting Standards Board (ASB)

  Replaced ASC on 1 August 1990
  Issues standards on own authority
  9 members – $\frac{2}{3}$ majority for approval of standard

- Urgent Issues Task Force (UITF)

  Sub-committee of ASB

  Assists ASB in areas where accounting standard exists but conflicti interpretations have developed

  Operates by seeking a voluntary consensus as to the accounti treatment that should be adopted

  Consensus pronouncements are known as *Abstracts*

- Review Panel

  Decides on revisions of defective accounts

  In 1992 the Review Panel started to issue statements about the accour of individual companies

  Examples of public reports include

  - Williams Holdings for showing exceptional items net of t and for calculating earnings per share on profits before, rath than after, exceptional items. Williams Holdings changed treatment for the subsequent interim accounts and stated that would also do the same in future accounts

  - Shield Group for treating a £3.5 million provision agai properties, investments and loans as a prior year adjustme Shield Group had to restate its accounts

---

Notes

Differences between the new standard setting procedure and the old

FRC more widely drawn than the CCAB

ASB issues standards on its own authority

Public companies have to disclose material departures from accounting standards

Review Panel aims to revise defective accounts

Big GAAP, little GAAP

Current debate as to whether small companies should have to apply the same generally accepted accounting principles as large companies, or perhaps should small companies be exempted from having to comply with accounting standards?

CCAB working party issued a consultative document in 1994 suggesting that all small companies except public interest companies should be exempted from nearly all SSAPs and FRSs.

Cost/benefit test should be applied to each compliance decision.

FRS 3 - REPORTING FINANCIAL PERFORMANCE

Introduction

Replaced SSAP 6 and amends SSAP 3: earnings per share now calculated *after* the effect of extraordinary items

Objective - highlight a range of important components of financial performance

tes

3.2 Format of profit and loss account

- ❑ Split into:

  Continuing operations (with acquisitions separately disclosed)
  Discontinued operations

- ❑ Only three exceptional items shown on face of profit and loss account remainder within statutory headings:

  Profit/loss on sale or termination of an operation
  Costs of a fundamental reorganisation or restructuring
  Profit/loss on sale of fixed assets

- ❑ Profit/loss on sale of revalued assets is:

Sale proceeds	X
Less NBV	(X)
	X

  ie, revaluation gain does not go to profits in the year

3.3 Definition of discontinued operations

- ❑ Sale/termination completed in the period or before the earlier of
  - three months of next period
  - date of approval of accounts
- ❑ If termination, activities have ceased permanently
- ❑ Sale/termination has a material effect on nature and focus of operations and represents a material reduction in operating facilities or turnover
- ❑ Assets, liabilities and results clearly distinguishable

Notes

CLASSIFICATION OF ITEMS

1 **Exceptional items**

are material

are within the ordinary activities

need to be disclosed to give a true and fair view

2 **Extraordinary items**

are material

are outside the ordinary activities

are not expected to recur

They are extremely rare indeed ie, they have been effectively banned.

3 **Prior period adjustments are**

material

applicable to prior periods.

shown in the statement of total recognised gains and losses.

OTHER STATEMENTS REQUIRED

4 **Statement of total recognised gains and losses**

Primary statement ie, it is necessary to give a true and fair view

Shows all gains and losses of shareholders in the year eg:

Profit from profit and loss account before dividends
Profit/loss on revaluations
Prior period adjustments
Foreign currency adjustments

---

tes

❑ Example

Statement of total recognised gains and losses for the year ended 3 June 19X3

	19X3	*19X2 as restated*
	£'000	£'000
Profit for the financial year	29	7
Unrealised surplus on revaluation of properties	4	6
Unrealised (loss)/gain on trade investment	(3)	7
	30	20
Currency translation differences on foreign currency net investments	(2)	5
Total recognised gains and losses relating to the year	28	25
Prior year adjustment (as explained in note X)	(10)	
Total gains and losses recognised since last annual report	18	

Notes

2 Other statements in notes to the accounts

Reconciliation of movements in shareholders' funds

Example

Reconciliation of movements in shareholders' funds for the year ended 30 June 19X3

	19X3	*19X2 as restated*
	£m	£m
Profit for the financial year	29	7
Dividends	(8)	(1)
	21	6
Other recognised gains and losses relating to the year (net)	(1)	18
New share capital subscribed	20	1
Goodwill written-off	(25)	-
Net addition to shareholders' funds	15	25
Opening shareholders' funds (originally £375m before deducting prior year adjustment of £10m)	365	340
Closing shareholders' funds	380	365

tes

- Note of historical cost profits and losses
- Example

Note of historical cost profits and losses for the year ended 30 Ju[ne] 19X3

	19X3	*19X2 as restate[d]*
	£m	£m
Reported profit on ordinary activities before taxation	45	13
Realisation of property revaluation gains of previous years	9	10
Difference between a historical cost depreciation charge and the actual depreciation charge of the year calculated on the revalued amount	5	4
Historical cost profit on ordinary activities before taxation	59	27
Historical cost profit for the year retained after taxation, minority interests, extraordinary items and dividends	35	20

Notes

SSAP 5 - ACCOUNTING FOR VALUE ADDED TAX

Company acts as collection agency for Customs and Excise

Turnover in profit and loss account excludes VAT

Costs exclude VAT unless VAT is not recoverable in which case include VAT in cost

SSAP 8 - THE TREATMENT OF TAXATION UNDER THE IMPUTATION SYSTEM IN THE ACCOUNTS OF COMPANIES

Accounting for income tax

Company does not pay income tax but acts as a collection agency for Inland Revenue

Income tax deducted from interest receipts, royalty receipts, therefore recoverable

Income tax deducted from interest payments, royalty payments, therefore payable to Inland Revenue

Show gross interest in profit and loss account

Unless question states otherwise, interest shown on trial balance or interest rate is gross amount

Contrast with dividends where dividend shown on trial balance or dividend rate is net amount

Accounting for corporation tax

Dividends paid are appropriations of profit. Therefore not allowed as deductions

---

tes

- Part of corporation tax (CT) charge is 'imputed' to dividends when pai
- Shareholders receive cash dividend plus tax credit (which is t imputed tax)
- Company pays ACT to Inland Revenue when dividend paid due to t tax credit attached to dividend
- ACT is payment of normal corporation tax in advance of normal d date for payment of corporation tax
- If high dividends in relation to taxable profits, ACT may not be capab of set off against CT in the near future

2.3 Profit and loss account disclosure

- Tax charge for the year

UK corporation tax at x% on profits for year
Over/under provision in prior years
Deferred taxation
Tax suffered on franked investment income
Irrecoverable ACT

2.4 Balance sheet disclosure

- Corporation tax payable (creditors)
- Deferred tax (provision for liabilities and charges)
- ACT recoverable on proposed dividend either netted off again deferred tax credit balance or shown under current assets

---

Notes

Corporation tax provision

Dr	Profit and loss	Cr	B/S

ACT on dividends paid

Cr	Cash/current liability	Dr	B/S
	Provision less ACT is		MCT

ACT on dividends proposed

Dr	Deferred tax or ACT recoverable or Profit and loss (if irrecoverable)	Cr	B/S

5 **Franked investment income**

Gross up investment income (credit)

Include tax credit in tax charge (debit)

Entry is therefore within the profit and loss account and does not affect balance sheet

ACCOUNTING FOR DEFERRED TAXATION

1 **Deferred tax and timing differences**

Definition of timing differences: accounting and tax treatments equivalent, but in different periods

Compare timing differences with permanent differences

otes

- ❑ Deferred tax: tax effect of timing differences
- ❑ Terminology: originating, reversing
- ❑ Effects: postpone or prepay taxation liabilities

3.2 Types of timing differences

- ❑ Short-term timing differences
- ❑ Fixed asset timing differences
- ❑ Revaluation surpluses on fixed assets
- ❑ Losses

3.3 Three possible bases for computing deferred tax

- ❑ Flowthrough

  No provision
  Profit unrealistic, liability omitted

- ❑ Full provision

  Provide on all timing differences
  Accruals priority
  EPS realistic
  Possible provision for liabilities not expected to crystallise

- ❑ Partial provision (SSAP 15)

  Provide if reversal expected

  Prudence priority

  Balance sheet liability realistic

  Subjective, requires budgets, EPS distorted, possible unprovid liabilities

---

Notes

.4 Two possible methods for computing deferred tax

- Liability method (SSAP 15)

  Rate at reversal
  Compatible with partial provision

- Deferral method

  Rate at origination
  Compatible with full provision

.5 Requirements of SSAP 15

- General principle: provide if and to the extent that a cumulative timing difference balance will be reduced at some year end in the foreseeable future

- Accelerated capital allowances

  Provide on maximum cumulative budgeted future reversal

  Standard working

  Revaluations: provide against revaluation reserve if rollover relief not available and disposal envisaged, otherwise disclose potential liability

- Disclosure in profit and loss account and balance sheet

  Amounts provided and unprovided split between major components

otes

Chapter 4 *Consolidated accounts*

1 INTRODUCTION TO CONSOLIDATED ACCOUNTS

Where a holding company has a subsidiary, CA85 requires the holding compar to produce 'group accounts' as well as its own company accounts. These grou accounts are usually in the form of consolidated accounts.

- Conceptually:

  Parent company (H) controls subsidiary (S)

  Parent and subsidiary act as single entity

  Reflect by showing position as if parent had purchased assets ar liabilities of subsidiary

- Relevant accounting standards

SSAP 1	Accounting for associated companies
SSAP 22	Accounting for goodwill
FRS 2	Accounting for subsidiary undertakings
FRS 6	Acquisitions and mergers
FRS 7	Fair values in acquisition accounting

2 THE BASIC BALANCE SHEET CONSOLIDATION

- Primary workings accounts

  Adjustment account (Adj a/c)
  Consolidated reserves (Cons Res)
  S Ltd reserves (S Res)
  Minority interests (MI)

Notes

PROCEDURE FOR BALANCE SHEET CONSOLIDATION

sic method

Amalgamate assets and liabilities

Cost of investment; Dr Adj a/c

Share capital

H to CBS
Group share of S to Adj a/c
Minority share of S to MI a/c

Reserves

H to Cons Res
S to S Res

Allocation of S Res

Group share pre-acquisition to Adj a/c
Group share, post acquisition to Cons Res
Minority share to MI a/c

Balance on Adj a/c is goodwill

Write off immediately to Cons Res, or
Capitalise and amortise (charge to Cons Res)

INTERCOMPANY ITEMS. INTRA-GROUP TRADING

Debtors and creditors/current a/cs should cancel

Differences due to

Stock in transit
Cash in transit

---

tes

- ❑ Adjust to eliminate differences

  Dr Group cash or stock
  Cr Current account

- ❑ Adjust for unrealised profit in stock in transit (see below)

5 UNREALISED INTERCOMPANY PROFITS

Stocks

- ❑ Calculate PURP on closing stocks from another group company

- ❑ PURP

  Set off vs CBS stocks

  Dr to Cons Res if H made sale

  Dr to S Res if S made sale (or split PURP between Cons Res and MI)

Fixed assets

❑	On sale:	Dr Cons Res (if H makes sale) Dr S Res (if S makes sale) Cr PURP a/c	with prof on sa
❑	Annually:	Dr PURP a/c Cr Cons Res (if H purchases) Cr S Res (if S purchases)	wi reduction i depreciatio charge neede
❑	At year end:	balance on PURP a/c set off vs CBS fixed assets	

Notes

PREFERENCE SHARES AND DEBENTURES IN SUBSIDIARIES

ference shares

Debit cost of prefs to the adjustment account

Allocate nominal value of prefs between H (to adjustment account) and minorities (to minority interests account)

Balance on adjustment account from prefs becomes part of the overall goodwill total arising on consolidation.

bentures in subsidiaries

Debit cost of debs to the adjustment account

Allocate nominal value of debs between H (to adjustment account) and outsiders (to creditors > 1 year, **not** to minority interests).

Again the balance on the adjustment account from debs becomes part of the overall goodwill arising.

DIVIDENDS AND DEBENTURE INTEREST OF SUBSIDIARIES

posed dividends of subsidiary

Cr to 'Dividend payable a/c'

Dr S Res if not yet proposed

Eliminate group share

Dr Dividend payable a/c

Cr (i) Cons Res if not yet recognised by H
(ii) Dividend receivable debtor otherwise

tes

- Balance on dividend payable account to CBS as 'proposed dividends minorities'

Debenture interest payable of subsidiary

- As dividends, except use 'interest payable a/c'

8 GOODWILL - ELIMINATION

Goodwill arising on consolidation is one example of purchased goodwill, whi must be accounted for in accordance with SSAP 22:

Normally write it off against reserves immediately on acquisition

But you may capitalise it as an intangible fixed asset and amortise it over expected life.

Notes

apter 5 Consolidation principles

GROUP ACCOUNTS

Entity concept

Account as if group one economic entity
Most common form

Proprietary concept

Different from entity concept only where there are minority interests

Emphasises ownership through the controlling shareholding

Parent company extension - minority interests shown as quasi-liabilities

Proportional consolidation - group share of individual assets and liabilities shown

CONSOLIDATED ACCOUNTS - FRS 2 AND CA89

bsidiary undertakings (CA89 and FRS 2)

finition

CA89 introduced new tests based on control

H owns a majority of votes, or

H is a member and controls board votes through rights to appoint or remove majority of directors, or

H is a member and pursuant to agreements with other shareholders controls a majority of votes, or

H has right to exercise dominant influence (provisions in memorandum or articles), or

---

tes

- H has a participating interest and

  (i) actually exercises dominant influence, or
  (ii) there is unified management.

Participating interest (CA89)

Means

- Shares, share options or convertible stock
- Held long term
- To secure a contribution to H's activities
- Holding of 20% or more

Formats of group accounts

- Balance sheet

  Minority interests must be shown either immediately after item 'Accruals and deferred income' or after item K 'Capital and reserves'.

- Profit and loss account

  Minority interests appear as an arabic numeral item between item 'Profit after tax' and item 15 'Extraordinary income'. Minorities' sha of extraordinary items would also be shown between items 18 and but this would be very rare indeed.

3 BUSINESS COMBINATIONS

3.1 The difference between an acquisition and a merger

- Viewed from group

  Merger: joining of related businesses with no member dominating
  Acquisition: assimilation of one business by another

Notes

Viewed from shareholders

Shareholders of merged entity are the same as shareholders of old entities ie, there is a share for share exchange

2 **Merger relief in the accounts of the holding company**

Ignore premium where 90% or more of shares are acquired by issue of equity

Individual company books - recording purchase of investment is dependent on treatment in consolidated accounts

Merger accounting

Dr Investment	X
Cr Share capital (NV)	X
Cr Cash*	X
* or any other part of consideration	

Acquisition accounting

- Use merger reserve where *merger relief is taken but acquisition accounting* used on consolidation
- Holds the 'premium' on the shares issued
- Used to write off consolidation goodwill

3 **Merger accounting in the consolidated accounts**

erger accounting

an alternative to acquisition accounting as a basis for preparing consolidated counts

use

Subject to satisfying certain legal conditions

Required in certain circumstances by FRS 6

---

tes

Legal conditions

Enacted in CA89

- Must obtain 90% or more of shares
- Parent must issue equity shares
- Fair value of non-equity must be 10% or less of nominal value equity issued
- Generally accepted principles must be met

All four conditions must be met

FRS 6 criteria

- No party is either acquirer or acquired
- All parties participate in establishing the management structure for t combined entity
- Combining entities are similar sizes
- Non-equity consideration is immaterial
- Nobody retains a material interest in the future performance of on part of the combined entity.

3.4 Comparison of consolidated accounts under acquisition accounti and merger accounting

	Merger method	*Acquisiti meth*
Pre-acquisition profits	None	Y
Fair value of assets	Not required	Y
Corresponding amounts	Adjust to include subsidiary	N adjust

Notes under
Merger accounting it is assumed that both company's have been merged since they were incorporated

hapter 6 Further consolidation principles

SSAP 22: ACCOUNTING FOR GOODWILL

1 Definition of goodwill

	£		£
Fair value of consideration	X	Fair value of separable net assets acquired	X
		Goodwill (bal)	X
	X		X

Fair value is now defined as in FRS 7 as the amount at which an asset or liability could be exchanged in an arm's length transaction between informed and willing parties, other than in a forced or liquidation sale.

2 Standard requirements

Non-purchased goodwill not recognised

Purchased goodwill

Recommend - immediate write off to reserves
May capitalise and amortise through profit and loss account

Negative goodwill must be credited immediately to reserves

3 Disclosure

SSAP 22 and FRS 6 together require detailed disclosures

Fair value table. For each class of assets and liabilities acquired

book values before the acquisition
fair value adjustments
fair values at the date of acquisition

otes

1.4 ED 47 proposes fundamental changes to SSAP 22

- Positive goodwill

  Intangible fixed asset

  Amortise through profit and loss account

  Economic life should not exceed 20 years (40 years in ra circumstances)

  Review life annually

  Only extend if relates to components at acquisition

  Review carrying value annually

- Negative goodwill

  Record as deferred income (bargain purchase) or provisic (disadvantages)

  Credit to profit and loss account over a suitable period

  Review fair values on acquisition to ensure they fully refle disadvantages

1.5 ASB

- No clear view as to whether ASB will develop ED 47 principles

2 FAIR VALUES IN ACQUISITION ACCOUNTING

2.1 Introduction

- SSAP 22 and FRS 6 both refer to 'fair value', but the definition given SSAP 22 is very basic. The ASB have developed guidance on how th fair value of an asset or liability should be ascertained in specif circumstances by issuing FRS 7.

Notes

Fair value is generally defined as the amount at which an asset or liability could be exchanged in an arm's length transaction between informed and willing parties, other than in a forced or liquidation sale.

Key requirements of FRS 7

The fair value exercise on acquiring an entity should be based on the assets and liabilities existing at the date of acquisition.

Liabilities acquired should not include provisions for future losses or reorganisation costs since these are post-acquisition matters.

Fair value of a non-monetary asset = the lower of replacement cost and recoverable amount ie, the value to the business (as in CCA)

Fair value of a monetary item = amount to be received/paid discounted, if appropriate, to their present values.

Impact of FRS 7

The main impact of FRS 7 in practice will be the banning of establishing a provision for future operating losses amongst the liabilities of an acquired entity.

3 VERTICAL AND MIXED GROUPS

3.1 Definitions

- **Vertical group**

eg,

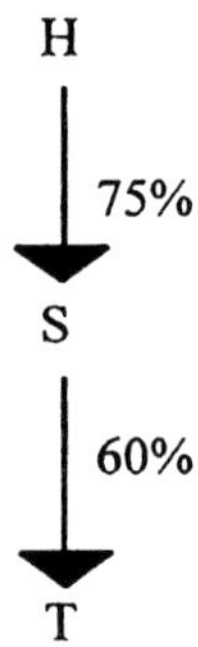

H controls S, S controls T, ∴ T is a subsidiary of H

- **Mixed group**

eg,

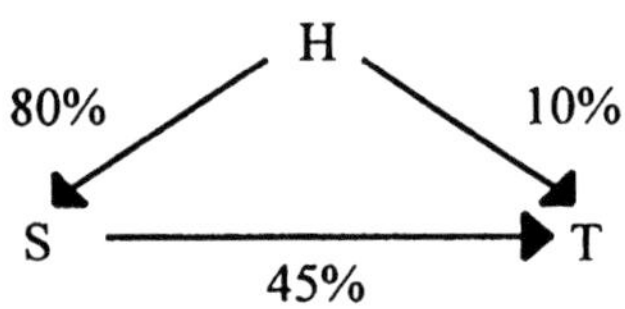

H controls S, H and S together control T, ∴ T is a subsidiary of H

Notes

.2 Mechanics of the consolidation

Direct method

Computes group accounts of holding company directly using effective interest of H in S to allocate share capital and Reserves

Indirect

Multi-stage consolidation
Sub-groups consolidated first

No difference in balance sheet assets and liabilities

No difference in gross turnover, costs

Differences may be

Goodwill
Minority interest

Indirect most often used in practice

Use direct method in exam (quicker)

otes

3.3 Examples

- Group chart eg,

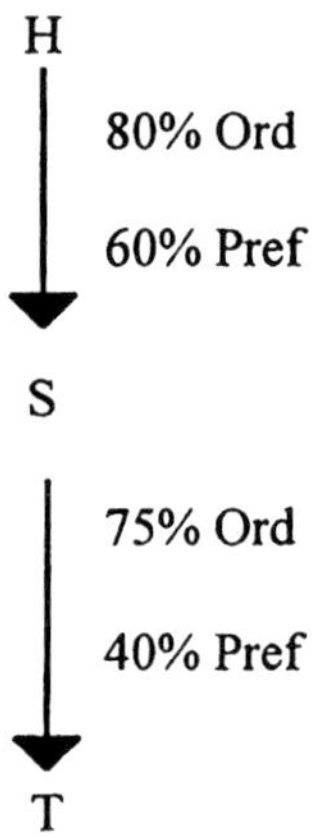

- Effective shareholdings

		S		*T*	
		Ord	*Pref*	*Ord*	*Pre*
Group	- Direct	80%	60%	-	
	- indirect	-	-	80% × 75% = 60%	80% × 40% = 32%
		80%	60%	60%	32%
Minority		20%	40%	40%	68%

- Cost of indirect investment — Dr Adj a/c : H's share (eg, 80%)
  Dr MI a/c : Minority share (eg, 20%

- Share capital and reserves: as per simple group but use effective share

---

Notes

Acquisition at different dates. Problem
Parent acquires subsidiary and subsidiary acquires sub-subsidiary on different dates
Acquisition date for sub-subsidiary?
Solution: use date parent gains control

Proposed dividends of subsidiary

eg,

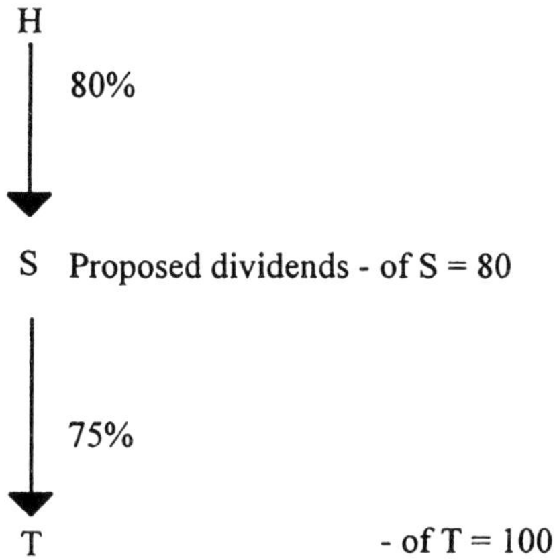

Dividend elimination account

	£		£
Cons Res (80% × 80)	64	Bal b/d - S	80
S Res (75% × 100)	75	- T	100
Bal c/d (CBS)	41		
	180		180

otes

Chapter 7 *Consolidated profit and loss, disposals, associates, exemptions and exclusions*

1 CONSOLIDATION WORKING PAPERS FOR THE PROF AND LOSS ACCOUNT

Basic objective

- To show the profit of the group as if it is a single entity

Basic technique

Add together the income and expenses of the holding company and i subsidiary undertakings. Exclude all intra-group items. Use a pro-form working

	H		*S*		*Adj*		*Consol*	
Turnover	X		X		(X)	(i)	X	
Cost of sales	(X)		(X)		(X)		(X)	(b fi
Gross profit	X		X		(X)	(ii)	X	
Distribution costs	(X)		(X)				(X)	
Admin expenses	(X)		(X)				(X)	
Operating profit	X		X				X	
Investment income	X	(iii)	X		(X)		X	
Interest payable	(X)		(X)	(iii)	X		(X)	
Profit on ords before tax	X		X				X	
Taxation	(X)		(X)				(X)	
Profit on ords after tax	X		X				X	
Minority interests			(X)	(iv)	X		(X)	

(i) Exclude intra-group sales

Notes

) ❑ Deduct unrealised profit. If S sold the stock MI need adjusting (later)

❑ If fixed assets are sold from one group company to another at a profit, remove the profit if sold in the current year. Base the depreciation charge on original value

i) ❑ Exclude dividends received from subsidiary undertakings

❑ Exclude intra-group interest payments

) Minority interests

❑	Share of S's pref dividends	X
	Share of S's post tax profits (after deducting total pref divis)	X
		X

Other points

❑ Dividends - H only

❑	H Ltd	X
	Group share of S's post acq profits	X
	Goodwill written off	(X)
	Consolidated reserves	X

If extraordinary item arises in books of S in year of acquisition include in the consolidated profit and loss account if it actually occurs post acquisition

cquisition of subsidiary during accounting period

Pro-rate the results of the subsidiary and only include the post-acquisition portion in the consolidated profit and loss account

otes

- FRS 3 disclosures required of turnover and profits of subsidiary

2 DISPOSAL OF SUBSIDIARIES

2.1 Consolidated profit and loss includes

- Pro-rated turnover, cost of sales etc, up to date of disposal
- FRS 3 disclosures probably mean that pro-rated amounts should be shown on face of profit and loss account under 'Discontinued activitie
- FRS 3 - profit/loss on sale is exceptional not extraordinary
- Gain on sale

The gain is

Sale proceeds	X
Less: Share of net assets at disposal*	(X
Less: Goodwill	(X
Group gain (exceptional item)	X

* For a disposal part way through the year, take

Share capital	X
Reserves b/d	X
Profits before appropriations pro-rated (× n/12)	X
Less: Dividends paid	(X
	X

Notes

N.B ENSURE THAT THE GROUP PROVIDES FOR TAX.
Payable by parent Coy on disposal.
(Sale proceeds – cost of investment) × Rate of Tax

Never pro-rate proposed dividends

2 Other points

Goodwill

FRS 2 requirement: Goodwill should be deducted from sale proceeds even if it has previously been written off to reserves

Computation

	£
Sale proceeds	X
Less: Share of net assets	(X)
Less: Goodwill not written off (Cr Balance sheet)	(X)
Less: Goodwill previously written off (Cr Opening reserves)	(X)
Group gain	X

Statement of reserves layout

	£
Group reserves b/d	X
Add: Reinstatement of goodwill	X
Retained profit for year	X
Group reserves c/d	X

Partial disposal

To calculate gain compare sale proceeds with share of net assets disposed of. Be careful with the percentages

otes

Example

A Ltd owns 90% of the shares in S Ltd. A Ltd disposed of a 10
holding

	£
Sale proceeds	X
Less: Share of net assets (10%)	(X)
Less: Goodwill (10%/90%)	(X)
	X

Subsidiary status retained

Example

A Ltd disposed of 1/3 of its 90% holding in S Ltd eight months throug
the year

Minority interest calculation

	£
$\frac{8}{12} \times 10\% \times$ £PAT	X
$\frac{4}{12} \times 40\% \times$ £PAT	X
	X

Subsidiary to associate

Example

C Ltd disposed of $\frac{1}{2}$ of its 90% holding in S Ltd eight months throug
the year

Notes

Include $\frac{8}{12}$ of turnover, cost of sales etc, calculating minority interests as — consolidate to date of disposal.

$\frac{8}{12} \times 10\% \times £PAT$ X

Then, take up

$\frac{4}{12} \times 45\% \times £PBT$ [∴ <50 - Not Subsidiary ∴ Equity Account]. X

→ Don't forget tax.

as 'income from interests in associated undertakings'

ASSOCIATED UNDERTAKINGS

1 CA 89 definition of an associated undertaking

Participating interest, and

Significant influence over operating and financial policies

Not subsidiaries or joint ventures

gnificant influence is assumed on a holding of 20% or more of the votes

se equity method

AP 1 definition of an associated undertaking

Long-term

Having regard to the other shareholdings, the investing group is in a position to exercise a significant influence.

Note: that the original SSAP 1 definition has been amended by the ASB's Interim Statement: Consolidated Accounts to bring it into line with the CA89. However an FRS on accounting for associated companies is still awaited from the ASB.

---

otes

3.2 Mechanics of the equity method of accounting

- Associate Coy

Consolidated profit and loss account: Include share of

- ❑ Profit before tax
- ❑ Tax
- ❑ Extraordinary items

Hence

- ❑ Exclude dividends from investment income
- ❑ No minority interests (except for indirect holdings)

Consolidated balance sheet

- ❑ Include share of net assets (including fair value adjustments) under fixed asset investments

Interests in undertakings

	£		£
Cost	X	Goodwill written off (to consolidated reserves)	X
Share of post-acquisition reserves (to consolidated reserves)	X	Balance c/d (share of net assets)	X
	X		X

Notes

EXEMPTIONS AND EXCLUSIONS

Parent company included in accounts of larger group

Wholly owned subsidiary, or

Parent owns more than 50% and no notice from other shareholders

Immediate parent must be in an EC state

The ultimate parent company's group accounts must be audited and comply with law of EC state

Small and medium sized groups

Not plcs, banks, insurance companies or FSA registered persons

Medium criteria are determining

	Gross *(before adjustments)*	*Net* *(after adjustments)*
Turnover	£13.44m	£11.2m
Balance sheet total	£6.72m	£5.6m
Employees	250	250

Gross is a simple aggregate

May qualify on either gross or net, so in practice group only calculates net where it fails on gross. Must satisfy two out of three in current and preceding year

tes

❑ **Excluded subsidiaries**

Reason	*CA89*	*FRS 2*	*Treatment*
Different activities	Mandatory	Mandatory (in exceptional circumstances only)	Equity accounting
Severe long-term restrictions	Optional	Mandatory	If restrictions in force at date of acquisition carry initially at cost. If restrictions came into force at a later date equit[y] account at date when restrictions came into force. Consider need for provisions for permanen[t] diminution in value.
Immaterial	Optional	Not applicable	-
Disproportionate expense or undue delay	Optional	Not permissible	-
Temporary investment	Optional	Mandatory	Current asset at the lower of cost and NRV

Notes

GROUP REORGANISATIONS

1 The legal structure of a group

e legal structure of a group will often reflect the group's management style:

Hierarchical managements will prefer a pyramid structure

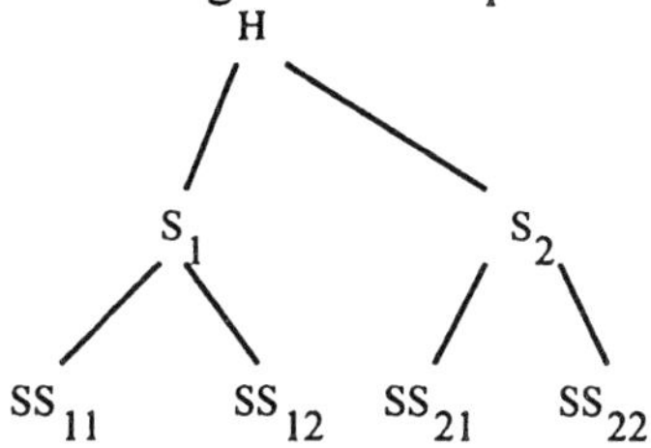

Progressive managements will prefer a flatter structure

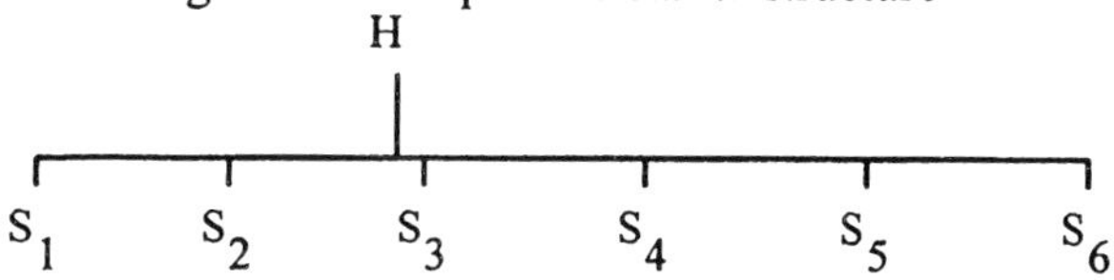

2 Demergers

Involves distribution of shares in demerged company to shareholders of old company

Shareholders therefore have two investments

Provides freedom to shareholders to sell or acquire stakes in part of former group

Can enhance shareholder value where old group undervalued by stock market

Example: break up of part of ICI to Zeneca

otes

Chapter 8 *Capital structure changes*

1 REDEMPTION AND PURCHASE OF OWN SHARES

1.1 Rules for the purchase/redemption

- Premium on redemption reduces distributable profits unless speci conditions apply
- Purchase out of distributable reserves or proceeds of fresh issue
- Transfer to CRR

Nominal value of shares	X
Proceeds of new issue	(X)
Amount to transfer	X

- Premium on redemption *may* reduce share premium account (instead distributable profits) if

  Original issue at a premium
  Fresh issue of shares has been made

- Reduction charged to share premium account limited to lower of

  Premium on original issue
  Current balance in share premium account

  Any remaining premium on redemption must then be charged distributable profits

1.2 Redemption out of capital

- Additional rules for private companies only

Notes

Calculation of transfer to CRR	£
Nominal value of shares	X
Proceeds of new issue	(X)
Permissible capital payment (PCP)	(X)
Amount to transfer	X

PCP	£
Redemption price	X
Distributable profits	(X)
Proceeds of new issue	(X)
PCP	X

REDUCTION OF SHARE CAPITAL

Examples of use: s135

Reduce/cancel liabilities on partly paid shares
Return capital in excess of company's needs
Cancel paid up capital no longer represented by assets

Cannot affect creditors' rights. If need to, use 'scheme of arrangement' as in a reconstruction

RECONSTRUCTION SCHEMES

Company in financial difficulty and wishes to raise further funds in order to survive. Therefore must:

Eliminate debit balance on profit and loss account to allow dividends to be paid once company returns to profit
Write off most of shareholders' capital as not represented by assets
Write off debts to achieve reasonable gearing ratio

tes

4 FRS 4: CAPITAL INSTRUMENTS

- ❑ Definition

  A capital instrument is any type of instrument such as a share or lo stock issued as a means of raising finance

- ❑ Need for a standard

  Increasing number and variety of capital instruments in recent yea has raised questions of how complex instruments should be accounte for

- ❑ Classifications of capital instruments

Item	*Analysed between*	
Shareholders' funds	Equity	Non equity
Minority interest	Equity interests in subs	Non equity interests in subs
Liabilities	Convertible	Not convertible

- ❑ Capital instruments = liabilities if they contain an obligation to transf cash or other resources

  This is consistent with the ASB Statement of Principles

- ❑ Convertible debt should be reported as a liability.

- ❑ Non equity - restricted right to dividends or are redeemable

- ❑ Liabilities initially recognised at amount received. Finance co (interest and premium on redemption): allocate to each accountin period so as to achieve constant rate on amount outstanding

---

Notes

apter 9 Pension costs and pension schemes

PENSION SCHEME FUNDING

1 Types of pension scheme

Defined benefit

Pension level contracted
Actuary calculates necessary contributions

Defined contribution

Contributions fixed
Pension depends on fund at retirement

2 Funded and unfunded schemes

Funded involve an external fund separate from the employer company

Unfunded involve no separate pool of assets

Funded schemes offer greater security to the employee.

3 Calculation of contributions: defined benefits

vo elements

Normal contributions: consistent ongoing contributions based on actuarial assumptions

Action to eliminate surpluses/deficits caused by (eg,)

Variation of assumptions from reality
Changes in assumptions
Changes in scheme terms and conditions

---

tes

2 PENSION FUND ACCOUNTING

2.1 Introduction

- SORP 1 contains the recommended contents and basis of preparati[on] for the annual report of a pension scheme. It is not specifica[lly] examinable but encapsulates best practice in the area.

2.2 Recommended contents of the annual report

- Audited accounts
- Actuarial report
- Investment report
- Overall commentary by the trustees

2.3 Recommended contents of the accounts

- Revenue account
- Net assets statement
- Reconciliation of the movement in the net assets

2.4 Other points

- Accounts should follow the accruals basis
- Investments should be shown at market value
- All other net assets should be shown on the basis of normal accountin[g] conventions.

3 ACCOUNTING FOR PENSION COSTS

3.1 Accounting objective of SSAP 24

- Accruals: recognise cost on systematic and rational basis over perio[d]

Notes

during which benefit is derived from employee's service

2 Accounting: defined contribution schemes

Charge to profits is contributions payable in respect of period

3 Accounting: defined benefit schemes

Two elements

Regular pension cost

Aim for substantially level percentage of current and expected future pensionable payroll

Use suitable method/assumptions

Variations from regular cost

Basic - spread over remaining service lives of employees in scheme

Exceptions

- Refund - may credit to profit and loss account immediately
- Material deficit from event outside scope of actuarial assumptions - prudence: to profit and loss over shorter period than remaining service lives
- Surplus/deficit from significant reduction in scheme membership - follow cash effects

4 Disclosure

CA - disclose financial commitments (provided and not provided)

SSAP 24 requires the following disclosures

otes

- Defined contribution scheme

  nature of the scheme (ie, defined contribution)
  the accounting policy
  the pension cost charge for the period
  any outstanding or prepaid contributions at the balance sheet date

- Defined benefit scheme

  the nature of the scheme (ie, defined benefit)
  whether funded or unfunded
  accounting policy and funding policy
  details of actuarial valuation
  pension cost charge for the period
  provisions or prepayments in the balance sheet
  any deficiency on a current funding level basis
  any commitment to make additional payments
  accounting treatment of refunds made to the company
  effects of changes in pension arrangements

- Example disclosure for a defined benefit scheme

  XYZ plc
  Extract from notes to the accounts

  'The group operates a defined benefit pension scheme in the UK. Th costs are assessed on the advice of independent qualified actuaries. C the total pension costs of the group, £28 million relates to the U scheme.

  The latest actuarial valuation of the UK scheme was carried out as at 1 March 19X1, using the projected unit method.

  The significant actuarial assumptions used in the valuation were th future investment returns would be 10% pa, future salary and wag

Notes

increases would average 7% pa and pensions in course of payment would increase at 5% pa.

At the date of the latest valuation the market value of the assets of the UK scheme was £859 million and the actuarial value of the assets was sufficient to cover 132% of the benefits that had accrued to members, allowing for expected future increases in earnings. The ongoing pension cost to the company has been offset by the amortisation of that part of the surplus not used for improving benefits as a level percentage of net pensionable earnings over 12 years.'

otes

Chapter 10 Foreign currency translation

1 APPLICATION OF SSAP 20

SSAP 20 deals with two separate situations

- individual company stage; where a company has entered into a dire business transaction which is denominated in a foreign currency eg, has exported goods overseas where the foreign debtor will pay in h foreign currency
- operations conducted through a foreign entity; where a UK compan has an overseas subsidiary, associate or branch whose results must b expressed in sterling to be included in the sterling group accounts.

2 THE INDIVIDUAL COMPANY STAGE

2.1 SSAP 20 requirements

- SSAP 20 applies to transactions denominated in foreign currency
- Use exchange rate when transaction occurs except:

  If transaction to be settled at a contracted rate, use contracted rate

  If transaction covered by a related matching forward contract, rate c exchange in contract may be used
- No further retranslation of non-monetary assets (fixed asset, stock)
- Monetary assets and liabilities retranslated to closing rate of exchang at balance sheet date
- Exchange differences to profit and loss account

2.2 Hedging in individual company accounts

- Finance foreign equity investment by foreign currency loan(s)

Notes

Translate equity investment at closing rate. Offset difference with that arising on loan and net amount to reserves

Necessary conditions for hedging to be permitted:

in any accounting period exchange differences on the borrowings are offset only to the extent of differences on translating the investment (any excess must be dealt with in profit and loss account)

the foreign currency borrowings should not exceed the total cash that the investments are expected to be able to generate (dividends plus sale value)

the offset procedure should be applied consistently

the loans need not be in the same currency as the investment

the offset is available on any overseas equity investment (not merely subsidiary and associate relationships) financed by foreign borrowings.

THE CONSOLIDATED FINANCIAL STATEMENTS STAGE

1 **Two possible methods**

Temporal method

Translate items using exchange rate on date on which the transaction occurred

Monetary assets and liabilities are retranslated to rate of exchange at balance sheet date

Closing rate method

Translate items using exchange rate at balance sheet date

Profit and loss account may be translated at an average rate for the period

otes

3.2 When the temporal method must be used

- Affairs of subsidiary are closely interlinked with parent
- Currency of parent dominant currency for subsidiary
- Factors to consider

  Extent to which functioning of subsidiary directly dependent on paren
  Currency in which most transactions are denominated
  Major currency for financing structure

3.3 When the closing rate method must be used

- Interest of parent is in net investment. Therefore accounting shou follow economic reality
- Normal method for consolidation
- Use unless special circumstances of temporal method apply

4 OTHER MATTERS

4.1 Group hedging

- Similar to hedging in individual company accounts
- Retranslate loan to closing rate as usual
- Offset in reserves the exchange difference arising on retranslating th loan against the exchange difference arising on retranslating the n investment in the subsidiary

---

Notes

2 Conditions which must apply for group hedging

Using the closing rate method

Maximum offset is the difference arising on the investment

The total borrowings do not exceed the cash flows generated from the investment

The treatment is applied consistently

OT452 – SSAP 24 group accounts.

see (4)

otes

Chapter 11 ***Profit measurement***

1 STATEMENT OF PRINCIPLES

The ASB's Statement of Principles provides a coherent conceptual framewo for the issue of accounting standards. The chapters are individually issued draft form. ***Note:*** Chapter 5 is dealt with in the next chapter of these Notes.

2 CHAPTERS 1 AND 2

2.1 Chapter 1: The objective of financial statements

- Objective to provide information regarding financial positio performance and financial adaptability
- Given by primary statements
- Should be looked at as a whole together with any supplementa information

2.2 Chapter 2: Qualitative characteristics of financial statements

- Primary characteristics

  Relevance
  Reliability

  *(**Note:*** trade-off between relevance and reliability*)*

- Threshold quality: materiality
- Secondary characteristics

  Comparability
  Understandability

- Application of these characteristics should result in accounts that give true and fair view.

Notes

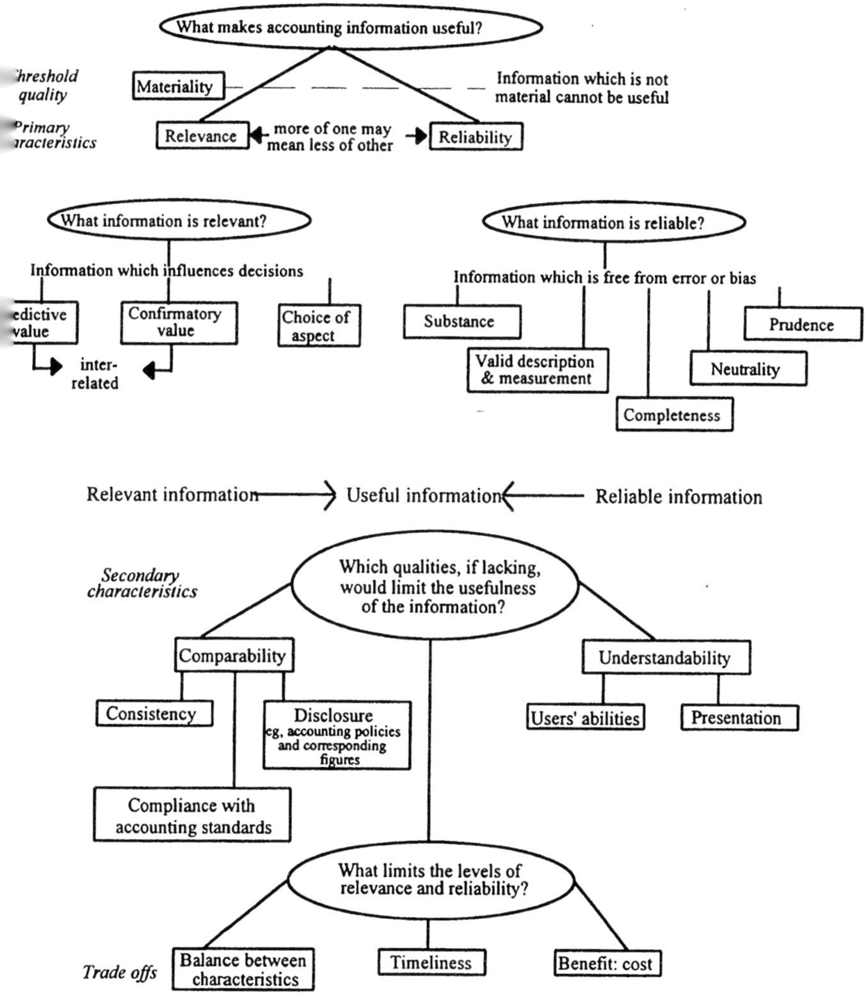
What makes accounting information useful?
hreshold quality
Materiality
Information which is not material cannot be useful
Primary racteristics
Relevance
more of one may mean less of other
Reliability
What information is relevant?
Information which influences decisions
edictive value
Confirmatory value
inter-related
Choice of aspect
What information is reliable?
Information which is free from error or bias
Substance
Valid description & measurement
Completeness
Neutrality
Prudence
Relevant information
Useful information
Reliable information
Secondary characteristics
Which qualities, if lacking, would limit the usefulness of the information?
Comparability
Consistency
Disclosure eg, accounting policies and corresponding figures
Compliance with accounting standards
Understandability
Users' abilities
Presentation
What limits the levels of relevance and reliability?
Trade offs
Balance between characteristics
Timeliness
Benefit: cost

otes

3 CHAPTERS 3 AND 4

3.1 Chapter 3: The elements of financial statements

- Seven elements
- Assets - Are rights or other access to future economic benefi
controlled by an entity as a result of past transactions or events
- Liabilities - Are an entity's obligations to transfer economic benefits
a result of past transactions or events
- Equity - Is the ownership interest in the entity
- Gains

  Are increases in equity, other than those relating to contributions fro
owners

  Revenue gains are those generally included in profit and loss
- Losses - Are decreases in equity, other than those relating
distributions to owners
- Contributions from owners - Are increases in equity resulting fro
investments made by owners in their capacity as owners
- Distributions to owners - Are decreases in equity resulting fro
transfers made to owners in their capacity as owners

3.2 Chapter 4: The recognition of items in financial statements

- Recognition means depicting an item in words (with addition
disclosure if necessary) and monetary amount within the primar
financial statements

Notes

General recognition criteria

Comes within Chapter 3 definitions of an element
Sufficient evidence that change in asset/liability has occurred
Can be measured at a monetary amount with sufficient reliability

CHAPTER 6

hapter 6: Presentation of financial information

The presentation decision is taken in the context of a structured set of financial statements comprising *primary statements* and *supporting notes*

Primary statements:

Profit and loss account (including a note of historical cost profits and losses)
Statement of total recognised gains and losses
Balance sheet
Cash flow statement

Features of financial statements

Aggregation
Classification
Structure
Articulation
Accounting policies
Notes to financial statements
Supplementary information

otes

5 CHAPTER 7

Chapter 7: the reporting entity

- Considers which entities should prepare financial statements, both individual entities and as parents (in group accounts)
- A parent-subsidiary relationship exists where one company contro another
- Basic principle

  An entity should prepare financial statements if there is a demand f that entity's financial statements and if it could supply financi statements that would fulfil that demand
- Consolidated financial statements reflect a parent's control of the asse and liabilities of its subsidiaries by the process of consolidation
- The investor should account only for its share of the results and n assets of its associates and joint ventures because control does not exis just the exercise of significant influence over their businesses

6 PROBLEMS OF PROFIT MEASUREMENT AN ALTERNATIVE APPROACHES

The accountancy profession's proposals for showing the effects of changin prices on financial statements have concentrated on two main systems, CPP an CCA. These are examined later

7 VALUATION OF ASSETS: ALTERNATIVE BASES

The CA85 permits either historical cost accounting or an alternative basis to b used.

- Use either historical cost accounting rules or alternative accountin rules for any asset

---

Notes

Historical cost AR

Fixed assets. Cost less depreciation
Current assets. Lower of cost and NRV

Alternative AR

Fixed assets

- Tangible: market value or current cost
- Intangible: current cost
- Investments: market value or other appropriate basis

Current assets. Investments and stock at current cost

otes

Chapter 12 Accounting for the effects of changing prices

1 PRINCIPLES OF CONSTANT PURCHASING POW ACCOUNTING

1.1 CPP accounts

- Conversion is to year end price levels (CPP units)
- Conversion factor

$$\text{Item} \times \frac{\text{Price index at year end}}{\text{Price index at origination of item}}$$

- Example: If year end 31/12/X8, sale made 30/6/X8, uplift to 31/12/X

  Depreciation charge where asset purchased 31/12/X4, uplift for pri change from 31/12/X4 to 31/12/X8

- Non-monetary assets: uplift as for profit and loss account items usi conversion factor above
- Monetary items already stated at current purchasing power: therefo no adjustment
- Opening shareholders' funds: uplift by price change in year
- Residual figure is total gain/loss for period

1.2 Evaluation of the CPP model

- Advantages
  Stable monetary unit used
  Comparison of data over time (as common unit of measurement)
  Better comparison between entities
  Gain/loss to shareholders of effect of inflation on their investment measured
  Less subjective than CCA (uses general not specific price changes)

Notes

Disadvantages

Not easily understood as to meaning of resulting figures
Users prefer readily understandable unit of measurement
'Value' given to non-monetary assets is not useful information in its own right

PRINCIPLES OF CURRENT COST ACCOUNTING

1 Objective of CCA

CA aims to maintain the operating capability of a business by highlighting the pact of input price changes on the net operating assets of the business.

2 The four main current cost adjustments to the profit and loss account

Cost of sales adjustment

Takes the holding gain element out of profit

Stock item costs £50 1 January, is sold for £120 on 31 March, replacement stock costs £80 on 1 April

	£
Historical cost profit	70
Holding gain (80 - 50)	(30)
Current cost profit	40

The holding gain is treated as follows

Dr	Current cost profit and loss account	£30	
Cr	Current cost reserve		£30

otes

- Depreciation adjustment

Aim is to charge to profit and loss account sufficient sums to enable t replacement of the asset

Historic cost of asset 1/1/X5		£10,000
Current cost 31/12/X6	£15,000	

Asset has five year lifespan

	19X
	£
Historical cost depreciation	2,0
Current cost depreciation	3,0
Depreciation adjustment	1,0

- MWCA

Computes gain/loss from monetary working capital

In period of rising prices, cost if monetary assets, gain if moneta liability

Computation

$$\frac{\text{Average index for period}}{\text{Index when typical monetary item originated}}$$

Stock index normally most appropriate as MWC levels relate to buyin and selling of stock

If opening debtors less creditors £5,000
Closing debtors less creditors £3,000
Index - average 200, opening 195, closing 203

Notes

		Charge
		£
$£5,000 \times \frac{200}{195} = 5,128$		128
$£3,000 \times \frac{200}{203} = 2,956$		44
Charge for period		172

Gearing adjustment

Computes proportion of above charges accruing to shareholders (less than the full amount of the charges because of borrowings).

Computation. $\text{Realised holding gains} \times \frac{\text{Ave net borrowings}}{\text{Ave net operating assets}}$

3 **Example current cost profit and loss account**

		£	£
Historical cost profit before interest and tax			X
Less:	Depreciation adjustment	X	
	Cost of sales adjustment	X	
	Monetary working capital adjustment	X	
			X
Current cost operating profit			X
Less:	Interest payable	X	
	Tax	X	
		X	

tes

Add:	Gearing adjustment	(X)	
			X
Current cost profit attributable to shareholders			X
Less:	Dividends		(X)

2.4 The current cost balance sheet

- Assets and liabilities are shown at their value to the business = th deprival value = their current cost

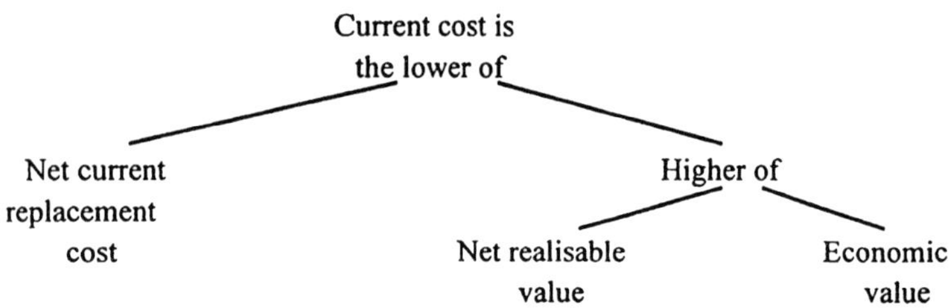

- This means restating non-monetary items (fixed assets, stock, e while monetary items remain at the same value as in the historical c balance sheet.

- Reserves on the current cost balance sheet will include a current c reserve

Notes

Evaluation of CCA

Advantages:

Computes operating profit after maintaining the operating capacity of the business

Relevant to real world business decisions re maintenance of business operations

Assets shown at current value to the business

Better comparison between entities

Disadvantages:

Values can be misunderstood

Increased subjectivity involved in valuations

Gain/loss to shareholders of purchasing power of their investment not shown

Many commentators unhappy with MWCA

RECENT DEVELOPMENTS IN ACCOUNTING FOR CHANGING PRICES

The ASC Handbook

e ASC produced a Handbook: Accounting for the effects of changing prices 1986, which identified the eight possible ways of combining the three ·iables in the alternative approaches to measuring profit:

tes

	Asset valuation (cost)	*Capital maintenance concept*	*Unit of measurement*	*System of accounting*
1	HC	FCM	£	HCA
2	HC	FCM	CPP	CPP
3	HC	OCM	£	
4	HC	OCM	CPP	
5	CC	FCM	£	RTA
6	CC	FCM	CPP	
7	CC	OCM	£	CCA
8	CC	OCM	CPP	

HCA, CPP and CCA have been examined above. RTA is a new propos[al] combining financial capital maintenance (FCM) with current cost asset values.

The total real terms profit earned in a year can be calculated in a table [as] follows:

IP Ltd

Adjusted earnings statement year ended 19X5

		£'000	£'000
Historical cost profit after taxation			552
Add:	(a) Unrealised holding gains arising during the year	249	
Less:	(b) Inflation adjustment to shareholders' funds	516	
Real holding loss			(267)
Total real gains			285

Notes

: Chapter 5 of the ASB's Statement of Principles

apter 5 'Measurement in financial statements' was issued in draft form in 93.

Chapter discusses advantages/disadvantages of alternative valuation bases:

entry values
exit values
value to the business

Total recognised gains and losses need to be split between 'operating profit' and 'other'

Operating profit is quantified by reference to capital maintenance concept used

otes

Chapter 13 Tangible and intangible fixed assets

1 SSAP 12 - ACCOUNTING FOR DEPRECIATION

1.1 Definitions

- Fixed asset - Those assets which are intended for use on a continui basis in the business.

- Depreciation - The measure of the wearing out, consumption or oth reduction in the useful economic life of a fixed asset whether arisi from use, effluxion of time, or obsolescence through technological market changes.

1.2 Required accounting

- Depreciation should be charged 'as fairly as possible'.

- The depreciation charge in the profit and loss account should be bas on the carrying amount in the balance sheet

- Realistic asset lives should be used

- Useful economic lives should be reviewed regularly and, whe necessary, revised

- Assets should be written down to recoverable amount if this is less tha net book value (prudence concept)

- Freehold land normally does not require depreciation; freeho buildings normally do require depreciation.

2 REVALUATION OF ASSETS

- Basis of valuation

  If revalued, SSAP 12 fixed assets would normally be valued at a existing use valuation (going concern concept)

Notes

SSAP 19 requires investment properties to be valued at an open market valuation

Incorporation of the valuation in the accounts. There is currently no requirement for SSAP 12 assets (ie, those held for consumption) to be revalued

Surpluses and deficits arising on revaluation must be credited/debited to a revaluation reserve

FRS 3 requires the profit on disposal of a previously revalued asset to be calculated as the excess of the proceeds received over the revalued book value at the date of sale.

INVESTMENT PROPERTIES

:finition of investment property

Construction work completed

Held for investment potential

Exceptions:

Owned and occupied for own purposes
Let to another group company

:counting

Do not depreciate (Companies Act conflict)

Include in balance sheet at open market value (MV)

Disclose bases of valuation together with names or qualifications of valuer

Specific mention if employee or officer of the company performed the valuation

otes

- Changes in value taken to investment revaluation reserve, unless deficit on an individual investment property is expected to b permanent, in which case it should be charged in the profit and lo account of the period.

4 ED 51 - ACCOUNTING FOR FIXED ASSETS AN REVALUATIONS

4.1 Contents of ED 51

This covers a whole range of principles including the basic areas of

- Asset recognition (as per Chapter 4 of the Statement of Principles)
- Cost ascertainment (similar to SSAP 9)
- Capitalisation of interest (see below)
- Enhancements
- Valuations

4.2 Valuation principles

- For each class of fixed asset directors should determine whether to carry that class at:

  Cost
  Or valuation

- Valuations should be:

  Open market value
  Not more than five years previously

4.3 Transfer from current assets to fixed assets

- UITF Abstract 5 requires that where assets are transferred from current

---

Notes

to fixed, the transfer should be made at the lower of cost and net realisable value. Pre-transfer losses should be charged against profits rather than be debited against revaluation reserve

CAPITALISATION OF INTEREST

guments for

Part of total costs incurred in bringing a fixed asset into use

Different results (PBT) depending on whether companies acquire or construct

Greater degree of comparability

guments against

Inconsistencies

Borrowing costs generally support the whole activities

Similar fixed assets may have different carrying amounts

rrently there is no UK accounting standard dealing with the topic, so UK npanies have a choice as to whether to capitalise or not to capitalise interest. wever once the choice has been made it must be applied consistently.

SSAP 4 - ACCOUNTING FOR GOVERNMENT GRANTS

General recognition principles

Prudence

Matching

Revenue grants

Should be credited to profits on the same basis as the expenditure to which they are intended to contribute is charged

---

tes

6.3 Capital grants

- Two treatments permitted by SSAP 4

  Credit against the cost of the asset and depreciate the net amount

  Treat as a deferred credit

- The first of these is believed to be contrary to the CA85, so compan: must adopt the second method.

7 INTANGIBLE ASSETS

7.1 ED 52: Accounting for intangible fixed assets

Only recognise intangible assets if

- General recognition criteria are satisfied
- Costs of creation are known
- Characteristics distinguishable from goodwill
- Costs measured independently of goodwill

Brands

- Wider than a trade name
- Seldom sold separately
- Factors similar to goodwill
- Therefore should be subsumed within goodwill and accounted f accordingly

Valuation

- May be carried at a valuation based on depreciated replacement co (DRC)

Notes

DRC represents CC (deprival value) of the asset

nortisation proposed on ED 47 basis

Maximum 20 years

Exceptionally 40 years

Annual review of amortisation period

CAPITALISATION OF RESEARCH AND DEVELOPMENT

finitions

Pure research. Experimental/theoretical work undertaken primarily to acquire new scientific/technical knowledge for its own sake

Applied research. Original/critical investigation undertaken to gain new scientific/technical knowledge and directed towards a specific practical aim/objective

Development. Use of scientific/technical knowledge to produce new or substantially improved materials, devices, products or services

counting problem centres on the conflict between accruals and prudence

counting treatment

Fixed assets purchased for R&D purposes written off over useful economic life

Research costs (pure or applied): written off

Development costs: may capitalise if conditions are met

pitalisation of development costs

Defined project
Identifiable costs

---

tes

- Technically and commercially viable
- Future revenues exceed costs
- Adequate resources exist

Disclosure

- Total charged to profit and loss (plc's and large companies only) sp between costs and amortised
- Movements on deferred development expenditure during the year

---

Notes

apter 14 *Leases and hire purchase*

ACCOUNTING FOR LEASES AND HIRE PURCHASE

ance lease

Definition:	substantially all risks and rewards of ownership transferred to lessee
Risks:	bearing of the capital cost and therefore exposure to - Unsatisfactory performance - Obsolescence - Idle capacity - Loss of realisable value
Rewards:	Primarily the right to unencumbered long-term use
90% test:	finance lease presumed if present value of minimum lease payments calculated using rate of interest implicit in lease amounts to 90% or more of fair value of leased asset

erating lease

Definition:	an operating lease is any lease that does not satisfy the conditions to be a finance lease

ACCOUNTING FOR LESSEES AND HIRERS

Finance leases

itially

Record finance lease both as asset (fixed) and liability ('net obligation under finance leases')

Amount to record is present value of minimum lease payments (fair value as approximation)

---

tes

Subsequently: asset

- Depreciate over shorter of useful life or lease term

Subsequently: liability

- Reduce by capital element of lease rentals

Profit and loss account charges

- Depreciation on leased asset
- Finance charges: interest element of lease rentals

Allocation of finance charges to periods

- Total finance charges

  Minimum lease payments
  Amount capitalised (

  Finance charges

- Objective. Constant periodic rate of charge on remaining obligation
- Options available

  Actuarial (pre-tax) - objective fully met
  Sum of digits - good approximation
  Straight line - small leases only

Notes

llocation of finance charges to rentals

Rentals in arrears

Finance charges are for period just ended

Rentals in advance

Finance charges are for previous period
Initial rental is all capital
At each period end have accrual for period's finance charges

2 Operating leases

Accounting follows strict legal form

No asset is recorded by the lessee

Lease is treated as simple rental

3 HP contracts

HP contracts of a financing nature should be accounted for as per finance leases (except depreciation by purchaser is over useful life without restriction)

Other HP contracts should be accounted for as per operating leases

otes

2.4 Summary

	Hire purchase	*Finance leases*	*Operating leases*
P/L account	(a) Depreciation (b) Finance charge	(a) Depreciation (b) Finance charge	Rental payments
Balance sheet - asset - liability	Fixed asset less depreciation Obligations under hire purchase contracts	Fixed asset less depreciation Obligations under finance leases.	- -

3 ACCOUNTING FOR LESSORS AND FINANCE COMPANIES

3.1 Finance leases

Initially

- Record lease as a debtor: net investment in lease
- Amount to record is cost of asset being leased

Subsequently

- Rentals received split between interest receivable (profit and loss) ar reduction of amount owing
- Split computed on various bases:

  actuarial (post tax)
  investment period method
  and variants

Notes

All methods designed to give constant periodic rate of return on net **cash** investment in the lease

HP contracts

ually finance charges can be calculated on the basis of the net investment in contract, so that the entries in the finance company's accounts will be a rror image of the entries in the hirer's accounts.

Summary

	Finance leases	**Operating leases**
Balance sheet	Net investment in finance lea	Property held for operati leases (cost - depreciatio
Profit and loss account	Finance charge (allocated on which gives constant periodic return on net cash investment	Rental income (straight-line basis) Depreciation

SALE AND LEASEBACK TRANSACTIONS

Definition

Where an owner sells an asset and immediately reacquires the right to use the asset by entering into a lease with the purchaser.

If the lease is an operating lease

The lessee **has** sold its control of the asset, so as long as the sale was at fair value, the profit/loss should be recognised immediately.

If the sale was above fair value - the excess profit should be spread over the shorter of the remainder of the lease term and the period to the next rent review (if any)

tes

- If the sale was below fair value:

  if a bad bargain, recognise the profit/loss immediately

  if to compensate for low rentals, recognise any profit immediately b spread any loss over the lease term

4.3 If the lease is a finance lease

- The lessee never disposes of his controlling interest so no profit/lo should be recognised. Any apparent profit or loss should be spre over the lease term.

Notes

apter 15 Other accounting standards and exposure drafts

STOCKS AND WORK-IN-PROGRESS

Stocks other than long-term contracts

wer of cost and NRV

Cost

Bringing stock to present location and condition
Cost of purchase
Cost of conversion
Production overhead based on normal level of activity

NRV

Actual or estimated selling price

Less: All costs to complete
All costs to be incurred in marketing, selling and distribution

luation methods

Acceptable under SSAP 9

FIFO
Unit cost
Average cost

certain circumstances

Standard cost
Adjusted selling price

Unacceptable under SSAP 9

LIFO
Replacement cost
Base stock

---

tes

1.2 Long-term contracts

Definition

SSAP 9 defines a long-term contract as 'a contract entered into for the desi manufacture or construction of a single substantial asset or the provision o service (or of a combination of assets or services which together constitut single project) where the time taken substantially to complete the contract such that the contract activity falls into different accounting periods.'

Calculation of attributable profit

- Sales basis
- Costs basis

Recognition of attributable profit/loss

- Only recognise profit when outcome assessable with reasona certainty
- Foreseeable losses should be recognised in full immediately

Recognition of attributable turnover for a year

- Value of work certified in the year
- Cost of work certified in the year plus attributable profit for the year
- Percentage of completion of contract

In early years of a long term contract, when no profit can be foreseen, turnov = cost of sales ie, Nil profit

Balance sheet

- The amount by which recorded turnover exceeds 'payments on accou should be included in debtors: 'amounts recoverable on contracts'

Notes

Balance on 'payments on account' should be deducted from 'net cost less foreseeable losses'. If it exceeds that figure - include in creditors

Any provision for foreseeable losses exceeding 'net costs' should be included within 'provisions for liabilities and charges'

Disclose in the notes under the balance sheet heading 'stocks'

SSAP 17 - ACCOUNTING FOR POST BALANCE SHEET EVENTS

finitions

Adjusting

Conditions existing at balance sheet date
Adjusted by convention or statute

Non-adjusting

counting treatment

Adjusting items: put double entry through
Non-adjusting: disclose by means of note

amples

Adjusting

Fixed asset. A valuation which provides evidence of a permanent diminution of value

Stock. Sales proceeds after balance sheet date provide evidence of net realisable value at balance sheet date

Non-adjusting

Issues of shares

---

tes

Losses of assets as a result of catastrophe (eg, fire, flood)

Mergers and acquisitions

Disclose

- Non-adjusting events
- Window dressing

3 SSAP 18 - ACCOUNTING FOR CONTINGENCIES

Definition of a contingency

- Exists at the balance sheet date
- Outcome unclear

Treatment

Likelihood	*Assets*	*Liabilit*
Remote	Ignore	Ignc
Possible	Ignore	Disclo
Probable	Disclose	Accr

Disclosure

- Where disclosure is required (see table above), disclose:

  Nature of contingency
  Uncertainties expected to affect ultimate outcome
  Prudent estimate of financial effect

4 FRS 5: REPORTING THE SUBSTANCE OF TRANSACTIONS

- Financial statements should reflect the substance of the underlyi transactions
- Detailed disclosures no substitute for inclusion of item in accounts

---

Notes

Common features of transactions whose substance not readily apparent:

Separation of legal title from enjoyment of benefits and risks of asset
One of a series of transactions with commercial effect understandable only if all transactions looked at
Inclusions of options making it likely that options are exercised

Use Statement of Principles to determine inclusion of item in accounts

Additional disclosures may be required in order to give true and fair view

Vehicle companies (entity used in off balance sheet arrangement) - consolidate

Linked presentation:

Show gross asset and liability in same place on balance sheet
Allowable for certain non-recourse finance arrangements

Offset:

Show only the net asset/liability on the balance sheet
Allowable on certain types of bank balances and overdrafts

APPLICATION NOTES

RS 5 contains detailed application notes giving guidance on how the quirements of the FRS should be applied in five specific situations

Consignment stock. Where stock is held by one party but owned by another, the key factor is identifying who bears the risk of slow moving stock

Sale and purchase agreements. The key question is to decide whether the commercial effect is that of a sale or of a secured loan

---

otes

- Factoring of debts. The key question is who bears the risk of slo payment and the benefit of early payment by the debtors
- Securitised assets. Show under a linked presentation if the necessa conditions are satisfied
- Loan transfers. Apply the same principles as for securitised assets.

6 ED 55 - ACCOUNTING FOR INVESTMENTS

Fixed asset investments

- At either cost or revaluation as with other fixed assets
- Current asset investments split between:

  Readily marketable investments
  Other current asset investments

- Readily marketable investments 'marked to market' at balance she date
- Gains/losses taken to P&L account
- Contravenes CA85 re valuation rules for current assets

7 FRED 8 - RELATED PARTY TRANSACTIONS

7.1 Definition of related parties

- One party has control of the other; or
- one party has significant influence over the other; or
- the parties are controlled by the same source; or
- one party is controlled while the other is significantly influenced by th same source

Notes

Required disclosures

All material related party transactions

The name of the party controlling the reporting entity

If different, the name of the ultimate controlling party

---

tes

Chapter 16 Interpretation of accounts

1 ADVANCED ASPECTS OF THE INTERPRETATION C ACCOUNTS

1.1 User groups interested in interpretation of accounts

User		Purposes	Information	
1	Management	Control costs, profits	(a)	Operating ra
2	Shareholders a investment analysts	Investment decisions buying and selling shares.	(b)	Stock excha ratios.
			(c)	Solvency rat
3	Lenders	Borrowing and credi purposes.	(d)	Cash flow statements.
			(e)	Value-addec statements.

Notes

Structure of operating ratios

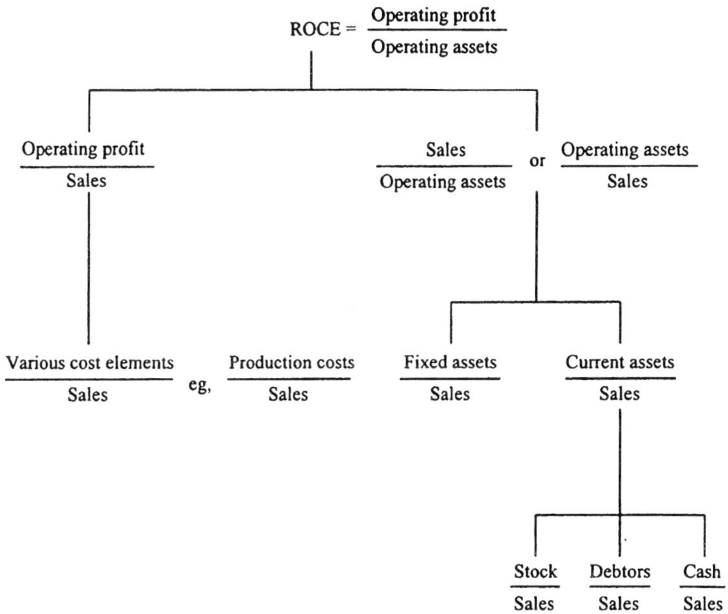

Return on capital employed

is is treated as the key ratio (or primary ratio), where the concern is with erating efficiency. Operating assets are related to operating profit.

r this purpose gross assets are compared to profit before tax and interest. This io is dependent on the profitability and assets of the company. Thus:

$$\text{Return on capital employed} = \frac{\text{Operating profit}}{\text{Operating assets}} \times 100$$

tes

2 SOLVENCY RATIOS

2.1 Short-term liquidity

Current/working capital ratio

- $\dfrac{\text{Current assets}}{\text{Current liabilities}}$
- Norm 2:1 but industry variation
- Low ratio may lead to insolvency
- High ratio may mean not maximising return on working capital
- Can be manipulated by window dressing

Liquidity, acid test or quick ratio

- $\dfrac{\text{Debtors} + \text{current asset investments} + \text{cash}}{\text{Short-term creditors}}$
- Measures more immediate position (ie, excludes stock)
- Norm 1:1 but industry specific
- Can be manipulated by window dressing

2.2 Longer-term liquidity

The gearing ratio is the most important

- $\dfrac{\text{Fixed return capital}}{\text{Equity capital and reserves}}$ or
- $\dfrac{\text{Fixed return capital}}{\text{Equity capital and reserves} + \text{Fixed return capital}}$

Notes

Denominator could be computed on assets side of balance sheet (total assets less current liabilities)

Can compute gearing from profit and loss point of view ie, interest cover

$$\frac{\text{Profit before interest paid}}{\text{Interest paid}}$$

Going concern models

Altman's Z score

$$Z = 1.2X_1 + 1.4X_2 + 3.3X_3 + 0.6X_4 + 1.0X_5$$

re $X_1 = \frac{\text{Working capital}}{\text{Total assets}}$

$$X_2 = \frac{\text{Retained earnings}}{\text{Total assets}}$$

$$X_3 = \frac{\text{Profit before interest and tax}}{\text{Total assets}}$$

$$X_4 = \frac{\text{Market capitalisation}}{\text{Book value of debts}}$$

$$X_5 = \frac{\text{Sales}}{\text{Total assets}}$$

pass mark for the Z-score is 3.0

Taffler

Developed for UK companies

Different combinations of ratios and coefficients for different business sectors

es

The model for quoted UK industrial corporates is:

$$Z = 0.53x_1 + 0.13x_2 + 0.18x_3 + 0.16x_4$$

where

$$x_1 = \frac{\text{Profit before tax}}{\text{Current liabilities}}$$

$$x_2 = \frac{\text{Current assets}}{\text{Total liabilities}}$$

$$x_3 = \frac{\text{Current liabilities}}{\text{Total assets}}$$

x_4 = No credit interval

x_1 measures profitability, x_2 working capital position, financial risk and x_4 liquidity

- Criticisms

  Lack of commonality of definition
  Retrospective information used
  No underlying theory (ratios used because they 'work')
  Little success in predicting time scale of failure

- Z scores are however widely used by

  Banks
  Local authorities (ie, supplier risk)
  Investment institutions to compare stock market risk with fundament risk

---

Notes

STOCK MARKET RATIOS

Dividend yield

Dividend yield

$$\frac{\text{Dividend per share} + \text{Tax credit}}{\text{Price per share}} \times 100 = \%$$

High dividend yield may mean:

Risky business
Stock market expects future dividends to be cut

Earnings per share - SSAP 3

lculation of basic EPS

Earnings

Group profit after tax, minority interests, extraordinary items and preference dividends

Divided by

Shares

Number of equity shares in issue and ranking for dividend

anges in capital structure

Issue at full price

Use a weighted average number of shares in the calculation

No adjustment required to corresponding EPS figures for the prior year

Bonus/scrip issue

Adjust number of shares by the bonus fraction for the period prior to

tes

the issue in the current period and throughout preceding accounti periods

- ❑ Bonus fraction = $\frac{\text{original shares and bonus issu}}{\text{original shares}}$

(iii) Rights issue

- ❑ Equivalent to a full price issue, followed by an immediate bonus issue
- ❑ Adjust the number of shares by the rights fraction in the period prior the issue for both the current and the prior year
- ❑ Rights fraction = $\frac{\text{cum rights price}}{\text{theoretical ex rights price (TERP}}$
- ❑ TERP will normally have to be calculated

eg, Welly plc announces a 3 for 5 rights issue at a price of £2.80 per shar Prior to the rights issue the company's shares traded at £4.00 each

	No	*Value*	*Tot*
Cum rights	5	4.00	20.0
Rights	3	2.80	8.4
	8		28.4

TERP $\frac{28.40}{8}$ = 3.55

Rights fraction = $\frac{400}{355}$

Notes

closure

Face of profit and loss account
Usually in pence, to one decimal place
Note showing how figure calculated
Comparative required

t and nil distribution bases

Net basis shows irrecoverable ACT as part of tax charge

Nil basis shows irrecoverable ACT as part of dividend

Use net basis (agrees with SSAP 8) but also show nil basis if materially (> 10%) different

lly diluted EPS

Takes into account all potential dilutions of share capital

No comparative required if assumptions change

Only include a dilution in the fully diluted calculation if it reduces the EPS figure

Only disclose if materially lower (> 5%) than basic EPS

pes of dilution

Separate class of equity shares not ranking for dividend this year

Add these shares to the basic number of shares

Convertible debentures

Increase earnings by the loan interest saved, net of tax

Increase the number of shares by the maximum possible conversion

tes

- If some of the debentures are converted during the year, pro rate for t[he] period they are unconverted

(iii) Options/warrants

- Increase earnings by yield on 2½% consols, net of tax, available [on] later of

  First day of period
  Date options granted

- Increase shares by maximum shares available

3.3 Price/earnings ratio

- Defined as $\frac{\text{Price per share}}{\text{EPS}}$

- High PE ratio may mean

  Expectation of strong profit growth in future
  Current year earnings are abnormally low and are expected to recover

3.4 Dividend cover

- $\frac{\text{Profit available for ordinary shareholders}}{\text{Dividend}}$

- Indicator of security of future dividends

- Alternative calculation: $\frac{\text{Earnings per share}}{\text{Dividend per share}}$

3.5 Key share price indices

- FT-SE 100
- FT-SE Mid 250
- FT-SE Actuaries All-Share

Notes

apter 17 Cash flow statements

FRS 1: CASH FLOW STATEMENTS

jectives

Entities to report on a standard basis their cash generation/absorption

Standard headings:

Operating activities
Returns on investments and servicing of finance
Taxation
Investing activities
Financing

finitions

Cash:

In hand
Deposits repayable on demand

Cash equivalents:

Short-term highly liquid investments
Convertible into cash without notice
Acquired within three months of maturity date
Advances repayable within three months of date of advance

CLASSIFICATION OF CASH FLOWS

erating activities

Show net or gross

Note reconciling operating profit to net cash flow from operating activities

---

tes

- If all elements of working capital increase in period

Operating profit		
Add:	Depreciation	
Less:	Stock increase	(
Less:	Debtor increase	(
Add:	Creditor increase	
Net cash inflow from operating activities		

- Gross method (may be shown)

	£'0
Cash received from customers	
Cash payments to suppliers	(X
Cash paid to and on behalf of employees	(X
Other cash payments	(X
Net cash inflow from operating activities	

Contents of other headings

- Returns on investments

  Interest received plus income tax recovered
  Dividends received (net)

- Servicing of finance

  Interest paid plus income tax paid
  Dividends paid (net)
  Interest element of leases

Notes

Taxation (excluding VAT). Including payments of ACT

Investing activities. Receipts from sales of fixed assets

Financing

Receipts from issue of shares, debentures and other borrowings
Repayments of debentures and loans
Payments made to redeem or purchase own shares
The capital element of lease payments
Payments for expenses of share or debenture issues

CASH AND NON-CASH TRANSACTIONS

Cash transactions (and cash equivalents) are reported in the cash flow statement

Non-cash transactions are not reported in the cash flow statement. They should be disclosed in a note if disclosure is necessary for an understanding of the underlying transactions

GROUP CASH FLOW STATEMENTS

oups

Only include cash flows external to the group

Dividends paid to minority interests to be reported separately under 'returns on investments and servicing of finance'

For equity accounted entity only show actual cash flows between group and entity eg, dividends received from associate

quisitions and disposals

Amount paid or received shown in the cash flow statement should be net of any cash or cash equivalents transferred as part of the deal

tes

- ❑ Give summary of effects of acquisition or disposal in a note

  Should indicate:

  How much of the consideration was in form of cash and ca equivalents

  Amount of cash and cash equivalents transferred as part of the deal

5 FRS 1 AND SSAP 10

Weaknesses of SSAP 10

- ❑ No definition of funds
- ❑ Merely a rearrangement of items in profit and loss account and balan sheets
- ❑ No specific format
- ❑ Choice of treatment for acquisitions/disposals of subsidiaries

Advantages of FRS 1

- ❑ Definitions of cash and cash equivalents
- ❑ Provides new information not available from balance sheets and pro and loss accounts
- ❑ Assists users in forecasting future cash flows
- ❑ Enables a judgement to be made of the quality of the profit earned
- ❑ Cash flows can be used as an input into a business model

Notes

apter 18 Segmental reporting, trend analysis and business valuations

SEGMENTAL REPORTING

rpose of segmental reporting

Appreciate results and financial position

Aware of impact of changes in significant components

finitions

Class of business

Distinguishable component of entity providing a separate product/service or separate group of related products/services

Geographical segment

Individual country or group of countries

Origin of turnover

Geographical segment from which products/services supplied

Destination of turnover

Geographical segment to which products/services supplied

AP 25 disclosure requirements

For each class of business and geographical segment

Turnover - external customers
- other segments

Profit before tax

Net assets

---

tes

- Geographical segmentation by origin
- Geographical segmentation by destination
- Total amounts disclosed should agree with totals in financial stateme

2 TREND ANALYSIS

Historical summaries

- Accounts will often contain a five-year or ten-year historical summ of key figures from previous years

  Example

£ million	*1992*	*1991*	*1990*	*1989*	*1988*	*1*
Sales turnover	8,798	7,691	7,153	6,998	7,396	1,.
Profit on ordinary activities	1,286	1,316	1,164	1,406	1,145	
Taxation	197	258	337	398	204	
Profit after taxation	1,089	1,058	827	1,008	941	
Earnings per ordinary share – diluted	22.2p	21.7p	17.0p	22.3p	21.5p	2
Dividends (net)*	5.5p	11.0p	10.4p	8.5p	6.8p	1
Dividends (net) per ADR	31.2p	62.3p	58.9p	48.2p	38.5p	6

- Inflation can result in such summaries giving a misleading impressio
- The ASC Handbook recommends that historical summaries of curr cost information could be restated in units of constant purchasi power

Notes

ample

X plc historical summary

As reported					**£ million**
	19X1	*19X2*	*19X3*	*19X4*	*19X5*
Turnover	25,737	29,314	32,381	37,933	**40,986**
Current cost operating profit	2,460	2,930	3,289	3,901	**4,438**
Earnings per ordinary share	63.9p	39.4p	47.5p	76.8p	**87.4p**
Dividends per ordinary share	20.25p	20.25p	24.0p	30.0p	**34.0p**
Net assets at current cost	32,564	38,799	47,021	52,564	**56,163**
Adjusted for the average UK retail price index of:	295.0	320.4	335.1	351.8	**373.1**
Turnover	32,551	34,136	36,053	40,230	**40,986**
Current cost operating profit	3,111	3,412	3,662	4,137	**4,438**
Earnings per ordinary share	80.8p	45.9p	52.9p	81.4p	**87.4p**
Dividends per ordinary share	25.61p	23.58p	26.72p	31.82p	**34.0p**
Net assets at current cost	41,185	45,181	52,353	55,747	**56,163**

tes

3 VALUE ADDED STATEMENTS

Definition

- Value added is the wealth created by all parties to a business, norma[lly] shown as being turnover less materials and services bought in.

Value added statement

- Shows split of value added between 'interested parties'
- Relevant to all interested parties not just shareholders
- May reveal further opportunities for 'adding value'
- No mandatory format, so any format is acceptable

Example

Group value added statement

Funds available		£	£
Sales			23,397
Less:	Bought-in materials and services		12,923
Value added			10,474
Add:	Investment income		225
Total funds available for allocation			10,699

Notes

Applied in the following way

To employees:		
Wages, pensions and other benefits		6,215
To governments:		
Corporate taxes	1,430	
Rates	200	
		1,630
To providers of capital:		
Interest on loans	196	
Dividend to minority	248	
Dividends to Redland Ltd shareholders	348	
		792
Retained by the company and its subsidiaries:		
To pay for capital expenditure to replace existing assets, to expand working capital and for growth: Depreciation	1,197	
Retained earnings 813 + (300 – 248)	865	
		2,062
Total allocation of funds		10,699

tes

4 BUSINESS AND SHARE VALUATION ALTERNATIVES

	Method	
	Earnings yield	*Assets basis*
Share value	Earnings × P/E ratio	Net asset value
Required information	(1) Future earnings (2) P/E ratio expected	Asset and liability valuation
Advantages	Independent of management's dividend policy	Useful check on other methods
Problems	(1) Forecasting earnings (2) Deciding on P/E ratio (3) Subjectivity of earnings (4) Effect of inflation on earnings	(1) Assigning values to individual assets (2) Limited applicability

Notes

Suitable for	(1) Quoted companies (2) Shareholdings in private companies of a size which enables the holder to influence dividend policy (eg, 20% → 100% holding)	(1) Going concern basis - as a check on earnings yield method (2) Asset-stripping - useful information if assets are valued at disposal value

tes

Chapter 19 International regulation

1 COMPARATIVE ACCOUNTING SYSTEMS

USA

- Role of the SEC, FASB
- Interest in a conceptual framework

Japan

- Government regulates the form and content of published accou through legislation

France

- Government regulates accounting rigorously through a 'National Pla

Germany

- The tax system has considerable influence in how accounts are dra up

2 THE INTERNATIONAL REGULATORY FRAMEWORK

Advantages of closer harmonisation

- Multi-national companies

  Access to international finance
  Improved management control
  Greater efficiency
  Easier consolidation

- Investors - better comparisons between companies
- Allows international economic groupings eg, EC to work effectively

---

Notes

riers to harmonisation

Different legal systems

Cultural differences

Different user groups (tax authorities may be dominant user group. Therefore accounts biased to their needs)

Professional accounting bodies have varying influence

rnational bodies concerned with harmonisation

IASC

Approximately 100 members
Publishes accounting standards for world-wide observance
Promotes acceptance of standards
Cannot enforce its standards
Too many options (in order to increase acceptability)

IFAC (International Federation of Accountants)

Same membership as IASC
Various committees including IAPC (Auditing)
Does not set accounting standards but its work helps their acceptance

OECD (Organisation for Economic Co-operation and Development)

Established guidelines re disclosure for multi-national companies

UN

Special projects aimed at improving comparability

European Union

Issues company law directives (eg, 4th directive now in CA85 and 7th directive now in CA89)

---

tes

3 CURRENT DIFFERENCES IN ACCOUNTING POLICIES

- Goodwill

  IASC - Capitalise, amortise over 20 year max
  USA GAAP - Capitalise, amortise over 40 year max

- Extraordinary items

  IASC - No definition
  USA GAAP - Similar to FRS 3 (ie, UK has moved to US practice fr
  SSAP 6)

- Deferred tax

  IASC - Liability method, full provision. Partial provision is allowed
  an alternative
  USA GAAP - Liability method, full provision

- Fixed asset valuation

  IASC - Cost but valuation is allowed
  USA GAAP - Cost

- Development costs

  IASC - As SSAP 13
  USA GAAP - Write off

4 ENVIRONMENTAL ACCOUNTING ISSUES

Definition

- Environment accounting is disclosure of the effect that the busine operations have on its environment, with the aim of operating on environmentally sustainable basis.

Current situation

- Little enthusiasm from the ASB in developing standards in this area.

Notes